A Primary Source History of the Colony of
CONNECTICUT

ANN MALASPINA

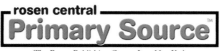
rosen central
Primary Source ™
The Rosen Publishing Group, Inc., New York

*For my mother, Doris Gould Malaspina,
whose ancestors—the Burrs and the Woodruffs—were among the early settlers of
Connecticut. Her happy memories of her grandparents' farm in Watertown
inspired me while writing this book.*

Published in 2006 by The Rosen Publishing Group, Inc.
29 East 21st Street, New York, NY 10010

Library of Congress Cataloging-in-Publication Data

Malaspina, Ann, 1957–
A primary source history of the colony of Connecticut/Ann Malaspina.—1st ed.
      p. cm.—(Primary sources of the thirteen colonies and the Lost Colony)
Includes bibliographical references and index.
ISBN 1-4042-0424-5 (lib. bdg.)
ISBN 1-4042-0665-5 (pbk. bdg.)
1. Connecticut—History—Colonial period, ca. 1600-1775—Juvenile literature. 2. Connecticut—History—1775-1865—Juvenile literature. 3. Connecticut—History—Colonial period, ca. 1600-1775—Sources—Juvenile literature. 4. Connecticut—History—1775-1865—Sources—Juvenile literature.
I. Title. II. Series.
F97.M35 2006
974.6æ02—dc22
                                                                    2005001392

Manufactured in the United States of America

On the front cover: American painter Frederic Edwin Church depicts Puritan minister Thomas Hooker with his followers in this nineteenth-century painting.

CONTENTS

INTRODUCTION

The Free Consent of the People

On July 12, 1776, the *Connecticut Gazette*, a newspaper in New London, published the Declaration of Independence. For the first time, the people of Connecticut could read the revolutionary document breaking all ties between the thirteen American colonies and Great Britain. "We hold these truths to be self-evident, that all men are created equal, that they are endowed by their Creator with certain unalienable Rights, that among these are Life, Liberty and the pursuit of Happiness.—That to secure these rights, Governments are instituted among Men, deriving their just powers from the consent of the governed," the declaration read. Connecticut citizens would no longer obey the laws nor pay the taxes of a government that gave them no voice.

According to Albert E. Van Dusen in his book *Connecticut*, a government that "deriv[ed] its just powers from the consent of the governed" was a precious idea for Connecticut's colonists. Thomas Hooker, the Puritan minister who founded Hartford, believed the power should lie "in the free consent of the people." In other words, people should elect their leaders and be able to limit their power. Hooker had left the Massachusetts Bay Colony in 1636, in part, to escape the overbearing authority of its government. In the wilderness along the Connecticut River, Hooker did not design a democratic government as we know it today. Slavery was not abolished in Connecticut until 1848, and women could not vote until 1920. Still, Hooker envisioned a society built upon respect for all people. Connecticut's first constitution, the Fundamental Orders of 1639, created a representative self-government, a radical step at the time.

The word Connecticut comes from the Algonquian Indian word, *Quinnehtukqut* (also spelled *Quinatucquet*), which means "Beside the Long Tidal River," a reference to the Connecticut River. In the early 1600s, Dutch explorers traded beaver furs with Algonquin tribes in the region. Soon after, English Puritans came to the Connecticut Valley in search of political and religious freedom, land, and a colony of their own. They built churches and gristmills, planted fields of tobacco and onions, founded colleges, and published newspapers. Ships built from Connecticut wood sailed from the colony's busy ports.

Tucked between the wealthier New York and Massachusetts Bay colonies, the small colony on Long Island Sound grew stronger. A determination to work hard carried it through difficult years. From the start, the colonists wanted to govern and support themselves, without interference from England. When the Revolutionary War broke out in 1775, they were quick to join the fight for independence. In time, the Connecticut colonists' belief in self-government, democracy, and individual rights would be the bedrock of a new nation.

CHAPTER 1

In the summer of 1636, a weary group of men, women, and children arrived at the banks of the Connecticut River. The Puritan minister, Thomas Hooker, had led them on a grueling westward journey from the Massachusetts Bay Colony. Carrying all of their belongings, they had trudged roughly 100 miles (161 kilometers), cutting through thick underbrush and scrambling over rocky hills. For nourishment, they drank milk from 160 cows, which they had led laboriously on ropes.

Settlement of the Connecticut River Valley

The English Puritans had left Massachusetts just two weeks earlier. Hooker was their spiritual leader, and his vision of a better future had inspired them to give up their homes and the lively society of the Massachusetts Bay Colony for an unexplored wilderness. Massachusetts was becoming too crowded; families needed farmland for crops and livestock. They left behind a strict Puritan government, which allowed little opportunity for their opinions to be considered. Hooker and his followers hoped to find the land and freedom for a new life.

Like thousands of Puritans in the 1630s, Hooker came to the New World seeking religious freedom. The Puritans, as their opponents called them, were at odds with the Church of England. Unlike the Pilgrims who settled Plymouth colony in 1620, the Puritans did not want to separate from the church. They wanted instead to simplify or purify it, but these ideas went against the British government with its close ties to the church. King Charles I and

British American clergyman Thomas Hooker (1586–1647) is pictured in this print traveling through the wilderness in 1636, with his Puritan followers from New Towne (Cambridge) in the Massachusetts Bay Colony to Hartford, Connecticut, the town he founded. Hooker is sometimes referred to as "the father of American democracy" because of his progressive views. He remained in Hartford and acted as the town's pastor until his death.

William Laud, his loyal Archbishop of Canterbury, believed the Puritans were dangerous rebels. Many had no choice but to flee England or face persecution. Some 1,000 Puritans, led by John Winthrop, founded the Massachusetts Bay Colony in 1630. Winthrop called his colony the "city upon a hill" in his sermon "A Model of Christian Charity," which he preached during the voyage to America, and said, "the eyes of all people are upon us." Thousands of Puritans poured into the colony, which was based on fundamental biblical principles.

Hooker was born in 1586, in Leicestershire, north of London, where his father was an overseer on an estate. When he was

This image depicts a group of Puritans beginning their voyage from the Netherlands to England, where they would assemble their group along with other farmers and tradesmen to settle in the New World. The Puritans had originally left England early in the 1600s after disagreeing with the Anglican Church. With the desire to worship as they pleased, and to practice a "purer" form of Christianity, they became one of the largest groups to settle New England, beginning in 1620.

eighteen years old, he enrolled in Cambridge University. Hooker experienced a religious conversion during his student years and became a Puritan. Ordained as a minister, he was an inspiring preacher. His strong beliefs set him at odds with the established Church of England. To avoid imprisonment, he fled to the Netherlands around 1630. In 1633, Hooker returned secretly to England, before setting sail for Boston.

Hooker's ship, the *Griffin*, pulled into Boston Harbor in 1633. He was made the pastor of the church in Newtowne (also

After his outspoken religious beliefs made him an outcast in the Massachusetts Bay Colony, former Puritan leader Roger Williams (1603–1683) was forced out. He fled to the region later known as Rhode Island where he founded Providence and began writing about the importance of religious freedom. In 1644, he consolidated his beliefs in a book called *The Bloudy Tenent of Persecution, for Cause of Conscience, Discussed in a Conference Between Truth and Peace*, the title page of which is shown here. Williams wrote, "God requireth not a uniformity of Religion to be inacted and inforced in any civill state; which inforced uniformity (sooner or later) is the greatest occasion of civill Warre."

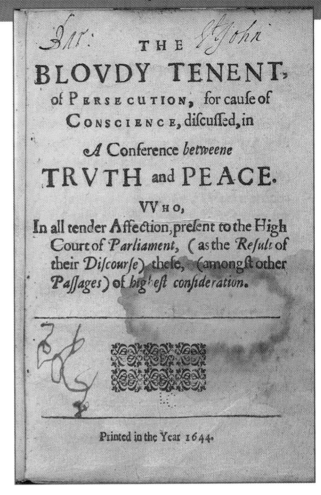

spelled New Towne), now Cambridge, across the Charles River from Boston. A respected minister, Hooker also participated in the government. For the most part, he agreed with Winthrop's policies. In 1635, he helped prosecute Roger Williams for his radical religious beliefs. Banished from Massachusetts, Williams founded the Rhode Island colony. In at least one area, Hooker disagreed with Winthrop. Hooker believed people should be able to choose their leaders and participate in their government. Winthrop felt the leaders knew best and should make decisions for the people. Perhaps Hooker's future, like Williams's, lay beyond Massachusetts.

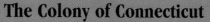

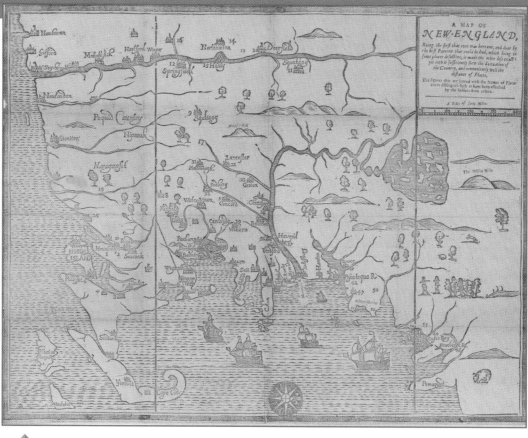

John Foster, considered America's first printmaker, created this map of New England in 1677, from a woodcut. The map's legend in the upper right-hand corner states, "the first that ever was here cut, and done by the best Pattern, that could be had, which being in some places defective, it made the other less exact: yet doth it sufficiently shew the Scituation of the Country, and conveniently well the distances of Places." This unsigned map represents west at the top and east at the bottom. Cape Code appears on the left and Rhode Island is shown literally as an island.

It is little wonder the English were drawn to Connecticut, the smallest colony after Rhode Island and Delaware. From its coastal plain on the Long Island Sound to its green northwestern hills, Connecticut held promise. The colonists set their sights on the Connecticut River, which flows about 410 miles (661 km) from northern New Hampshire to Long Island Sound. The wide river would be a major transportation route. Early plantations, or settlements, were established along its shores, and its valley was an agricultural heartland. Two other rivers, the Thames and the Housatonic, were navigable for transporting goods. Corn, rye, tobacco, and other basic crops grew well on the flood plains. Waterfalls provided energy for gristmills and sawmills.

The Connecticut coast on the Long Island Sound was suitable for fishing and maritime trade. Protected from Atlantic storms by Long Island, Connecticut's jagged shore, with many inlets, provided safe harbors. New London was the finest harbor, but smaller towns like Fairfield, Stamford, and Norwalk also launched ships filled with wood and cattle. Connecticut's rocky soil and thick forests were obstacles for the colonists. They struggled, using primitive tools, to fell trees and haul away stones to make way for settlements.

In the dense forests, colonists hunted white-tailed deer, squirrel, raccoon, turkey, and other animals for food and fur. Flocks of birds darkened the sky and were easy prey. Ducks summered on the lakes, and schools of fish filled the rivers and the sound. Salmon spawned in the rivers, and colonists dug oysters from tidal flats. Men were paid to kill wolves, which are major predators. In New London in 1648, according to Hamilton D. Hurd in his *History of New London County, Connecticut*, settlers declared, "he that kills the wolf shall have of everie familie in towne six pence conditionaly that he bring the head and the skin to any two of the townsmen."

Although Hooker is called the Father of Connecticut, Dutch traders and English settlers had come before him. In 1633, a small group of colonists sailed from Plymouth to settle where the Farmington River flows into the Connecticut River. The Podunk tribe wanted their help to defend against other tribes. Two years later, at least sixty Puritans from Dorchester,

Massachusetts, settled nearby. Early ice on the river that autumn sent many back to Massachusetts to avoid starvation, but some remained. The settlement, led by Roger Ludlow and Reverend John Warham, was named Windsor. Seeds from Virginia colony tobacco plantations were sown in Windsor's soil in 1640.

In 1634, the trader John Oldham and nine others from Watertown, Massachusetts, came to a bend in the Connecticut River a few miles south of the future Hartford. The Wongunk Indians traded beaver pelts with the newcomers. More families from Watertown, led by Puritan ministers Richard Denton and John Sherman, joined them in 1635. The settlers saw the marsh hay in the meadows and fertile soil above the river. They planted fields along the river, grazed cattle, and laid out a town with a central common, calling it Wethersfield.

Hooker's group arrived in 1636. It called its settlement Hartford, after Hertford, England, the home of one of Hooker's companions. Hartford became a center of trade and government. Later, it was Connecticut's capital. Windsor, Wethersfield, and Hartford were at first part of the Massachusetts Bay Colony, but the colonists would soon establish their own government.

To the colonists, Connecticut was a mysterious wilderness, but Algonquin Indians had inhabited the region for roughly 12,000 years. Connecticut tribes, such as the Tunxis and the Suckiaugs, referred to themselves as people of a specific place. Dozens of tribes hunted, fished, and farmed in small settlements. They shared a similar language and culture, but were often at war. This lack of unity, along with smallpox epidemics that killed entire villages in the 1630s, allowed the English to easily overpower them.

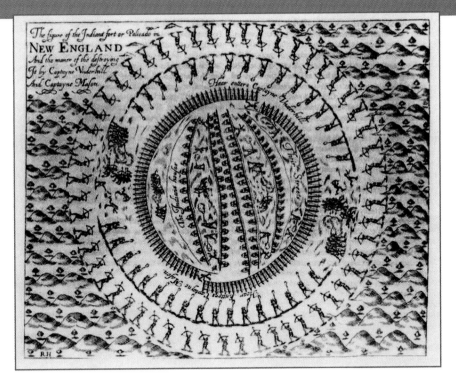

This engraving from 1638 depicts the Pequot Indian village called Fort Mystic that was attacked and destroyed by Captain John Underhill and Captain John Mason on May 26, 1637. As the fighting between the Pequot Indians and the Englishmen continued, Mason set fire to eighty huts. As many as 700 Native Americans died in one hour as a result of the fire and fighting, while two Englishmen were killed and twenty or thirty were wounded.

In the beginning, the Indians traded fur for metal, cloth, pottery, and glass, and sold their land for small amounts of goods. "The Indians, at their first settlement, performed many acts of kindness toward them [the settlers]. The Indians instructed colonists in the manner of planting and dressing the Indian corn. They carried them upon their backs, through rivers and waters," wrote Benjamin Trumbull in his 1898 book, *History of Connecticut.* But the Algonquins soon realized the colonists did not intend to share the land.

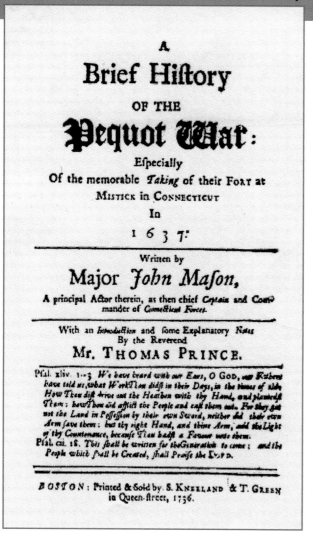

The title page of *A Brief History of the Pequot War: Especially of the Taking of the Fort at Mistick in Connecticut in 1637*, written by Captain John Mason several years after the conflict. Mason had been assigned the position of commanding the expedition to fight the Pequots by Connecticut's General Court. He also wrote an account of the conflict, *A Brief History of the Pequot War*, seen here, which outlined the American position on the fight for Native American lands. Even as early as 1637, most Americans believed they had a God-given right to Native American land in the New World. See page 53 for a transcription of an excerpt.

Tensions rose between the colonists and the Pequots near Narragansett Bay. According to some sources, Niantic Indians on Block Island in Long Island Sound killed John Oldham, the trader, during the summer of 1636. (Other sources indicate that Narragansett or Pequot tribes could have been responsible for his death.) The Pequots were suspected to have given refuge to the men responsible. Vowing revenge, Captain John Endicott of Boston sailed to Block Island. The Indians had largely fled, though Endicott managed to kill several of them before he burned empty villages. The Pequots retaliated by attacking Fort Saybrook, at the mouth of the Connecticut River and Wethersfield. The English declared war.

On May 26, 1637, the English surrounded the Pequot village at Mystic. They fired a volley at dawn then stormed the fort. The Pequots fought fiercely, but the English set fire to eighty huts. In a short time, 600 to 700 Pequots were dead, while just two English soldiers were killed. The war ended in September 1638, with the Treaty of Hartford, which banished Pequots from their territory. The survivors became slaves. The Pequots were "blotted out from heaven," wrote one Puritan in a 1643 account of the Pequot War. Hundreds of years would pass before the Pequots recaptured a fragment of what they lost. Meanwhile, Connecticut belonged to the colonists.

CHAPTER 2

The King's Charter

While the Connecticut Valley settlers cleared fields to plant their first corn crop, they were anxious to break free from Massachusetts. First, they had to settle a dispute with a group of eleven wealthy Puritan families in England. These merchants had claimed the land through a patent granted by the Crown to the Earl of Warwick in 1631. The colonists finally won permission to settle Connecticut. In May 1637, elections were held in Wethersfield, Windsor, and Hartford to select deputies and magistrates to serve in a General Court. The court's purpose was to decide how to best handle conflicts with Pequot tribes. Later, the men began to consider the best form of government for the new colony.

Their spiritual leader, Thomas Hooker, inspired them to look at government in a new way. On May 31, 1638, Hooker preached a powerful sermon to the General Court based on a passage in the Bible, "Take you wise men, and understanding, and known among your tribes, and I will make them rulers over you." Hooker outlined three doctrines: the choice of magistrates belongs to the people; the privilege of election belongs to the people; and those with the power to appoint their leaders should also set the boundaries of their power. In short, said Hooker in an excerpt of the Fundamental Orders, "the foundation of authority is laid in the free consent of the people." The colonists welcomed this new concept of government.

The General Court adopted the Fundamental Orders in January 1639. The document created an independent government

In 1639, the colonists of Windsor, Wethersfield, and Hartford formed one of America's first Constitutions, the Fundamental Orders of Connecticut, the first page of which is shown here. In total, the document outlined Connecticut's early system of independent government in a preamble and eleven basic laws. It set standards that called for a general assembly in the colony, the election of its officials, and the laws that controlled court proceedings. See page 53 for a transcription of the preamble and the first fundamental.

for Connecticut, with no mention of the British monarch. "To mayntayne the peace and union for such a people there should be an orderly and decent Government established according to God," it read. It began with a covenant, or promise, binding the three towns to obey the Fundamental Orders, and included eleven orders, or laws, based on the Bible. According to the document, all men who were capable of "honest conversation" could vote, provided that they were believers in the Trinity and were considered of good character. Although Connecticut did not limit the vote to Puritan leaders, it did exclude Quakers, Jews, and atheists. Church membership was not required for voting, but the system was not a true democracy. (According to the Charter of 1663, only white men who owned property and land worth at least 50 shillings could participate in government. Women, indentured servants, slaves, Native Americans, and men without property were excluded.) Still, the Fundamental Orders is often called the first constitution to establish a democratic government.

The colonists soon had laws. In 1650, Roger Ludlow, a lawyer, wrote Connecticut's first Code of Laws. It begins with a bill of rights, stating "that no mans life shall bee taken away, no mans honor or good name shall bee stained, no mans person shall be arrested . . . unless it bee by the vertue or equity of some express Law of the Country . . ." While protecting individual rights, the laws also governed behavior. People who swore, lied, or showed disrespect to the church often faced fines and time in the stocks, a wooden frame with holes for the feet and hands. Others who lied were whipped. Many people who committed discretions were humiliated in public when forced to wear a sign describing their crimes. Bachelors were not allowed to live alone. Idleness and stubbornness were prohibited.

On April 24, 1638, a ship carrying 500 English Puritans dropped anchor at the mouth of the Quinnipiac River on the northern shore of Long Island Sound. John Davenport, a Puritan clergyman, and Theophilus Eaton, a wealthy London merchant, led the group. Like Hooker, Davenport had fled England after disagreeing with the Church of England. After sailing to Boston, he was disheartened by religious infighting in Massachusetts and was disappointed that most of the best farmland had already been claimed. He set his eyes on Connecticut, but he wanted his own colony.

Eaton had gone earlier to explore the region and meet the Quinnipiac Indians. They welcomed the English settlers. Soon

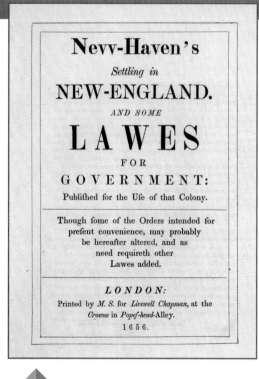

Puritan clergyman John Davenport (1597–1670) arrived in Connecticut with his boyhood friend Theophilus Eaton and a large group of colonists in 1638. Like Thomas Hooker, Davenport departed for America in the hopes of beginning a new religious colony with his followers. In April 1638, Davenport, Eaton, and their Puritan worshippers founded the colony of Quinnipiac (New Haven), where Davenport became head pastor of the New Haven church and Eaton became governor. Governor Eaton wrote laws for the colony in 1656, the first page of which is pictured.

after landing, Davenport held a service of worship on the first Sabbath under a spreading oak tree. In November, the Quinnipiac sachem (leader) agreed to sell the land in exchange for "twelve coats of English trucking cloth, twelve alchemy spoons, twelve hatchets, twelve hoes, two dozen knives, twelve porringers, and four cases of French knives and scissors." This exchange seems unfair today, but the goods were highly valued at the time.

Davenport and Eaton hoped to create a religious utopia, or perfect state, and a commercial empire to control Long Island Sound

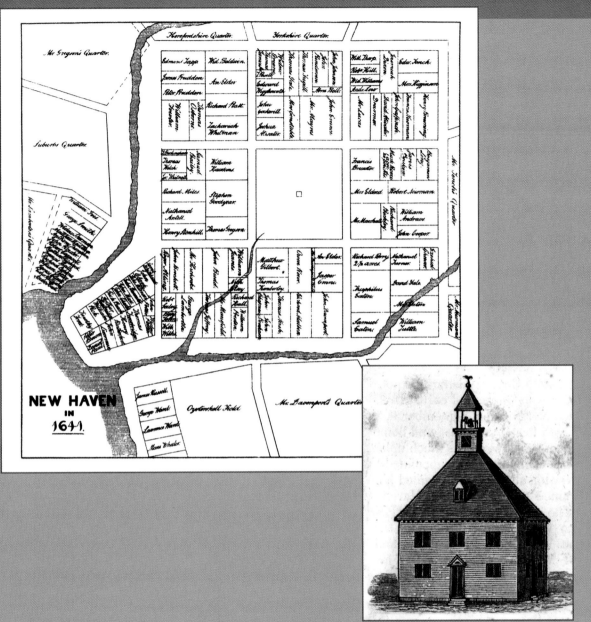

NEW HAVEN
IN
1641.

Despite the best of intentions and the hard work of its citizenry, the fledgling New Haven colony struggled to survive. Caught between the economic success of Boston and New Amsterdam, there was little need for a trading base on Long Island Sound. This seventeenth-century map of New Haven, showing the grid layout of the colony and the lots of its residents in nine squares, is known as the "Brockett Map." New Haven's First Meetinghouse, built in 1640, was centered in the green commons along with the colony's burial grounds, school, and three churches. In 1665, New Haven was included in the larger and more democratic Connecticut colony, even in the face of its citizens' efforts for it to remain independent.

and territory as far south as the Delaware Bay. By 1640, they had formed a government, established a church, and named the settlement Newhaven, later New Haven. Eaton was the first governor of this theocratic, or religious, colony. The colony would be "of such civil order as might be most pleasing unto GOD," stated its original 1639 constitution. Religious leaders formed the government and only a few men could vote, unlike in the Connecticut Colony.

By 1641, some 800 people lived in New Haven. The colony expanded to include Milford, Guilford, and Stamford, but New Haven was slow to prosper. Wedged between Boston and New Amsterdam, now New York City, New Haven could not establish a successful economy. Hoping to secure trade with England, the colonists, in 1647, launched the ship, filled with furs, grain, and lumber bound for England. It sank and was never found. New Haven's inflexible religious society would not last.

The news from England in 1660 was bad. The Puritans, led by Oliver Cromwell, had controlled England since 1649, when the monarchy lost a civil war and King Charles I was beheaded. After Cromwell's death in 1658, the Puritan government collapsed. In 1660, the son of Charles I, also named Charles, was restored to the throne. The Connecticut colonists feared that Charles II, who opposed the Puritans, might take away their self-rule. They had prospered for nearly thirty years without a royal charter to legally establish the colony and define the rights of the colonists. Now Connecticut's colonists needed a charter for protection.

John Winthrop Jr., Connecticut's governor, traveled to England in 1661, to negotiate with the British crown. Winthrop, a talented speaker and skilled diplomat, was well suited for the job. The eldest son of John Winthrop, Massachusetts's first governor, Winthrop was educated at Trinity College in Dublin, Ireland. He was trained as a lawyer, and knew many influential men in England. Winthrop had helped to found Saybrook, a small colony at the mouth of the Connecticut River, and the New London plantation. In 1657, Winthrop was elected governor of Connecticut.

Winthrop arrived in England in 1661, and enlisted wealthy Puritans to plead his case to the monarchy. Merchants who had helped Winthrop establish Saybrook supported their friend's request. Finally, King Charles II agreed to grant the charter on April 23, 1662, and Connecticut adopted it by October of that year.

New Haven wasn't the only colony struggling to survive. Threatened by Native Americans and competition from the Dutch in New Netherland, later New York, the New England colonies sharing Puritan beliefs looked to each other for support. In 1643, according to the Articles of Confederation of the United Colonies of New England, New Haven, Massachusetts, Plymouth, and Connecticut decided to "enter into a firm and perpetual league of friendship." This united confederation helped support the colonies through difficult years.

They needed each other in 1675, for instance, when war broke out between the Plymouth colony and its former friends, the Wampanoags. The Wampanoag sachem, Metacomet, known as King Philip, resented the loss of his land and authority to the colonists. According to author Joy Hakim in *Making Thirteen Colonies*, King Philip declared, "I am resolved not to see the day when I have no country." Connecticut sent men and supplies to support Plymouth in the bloody conflict, King Philip's War. According to Hakim, more than a dozen towns were burned, including Simsbury, Connecticut. Thousands of Native Americans were killed, along with hundreds of colonists. Fields—and livelihoods—were completely destroyed. The war ended any possibility that the two cultures could live in peace.

Because Connecticut's Fundamental Orders had no authority in England, the colony's leaders had to obtain a charter from the king of England that approved of its existence and its government. All of New England, including Connecticut, was claimed by Charles II, so the rights of the colonies were controlled by the Crown and were obtained by a royal charter. In 1661, John Winthrop Jr., was sent to England by Connecticut's General Court to gain the royal charter for the colony pictured here. See page 54 for an excerpt from the charter. The famous tree known as the Charter Oak is also shown above. It was the legendary hiding place of the colony's charter from Charles II.

Although the colonists now felt more secure, Connecticut had to fight to keep its charter after King James II succeeded his brother to the throne in 1685. Seeking control over the colonies, the king appointed Sir Edmund Andros to take charge of New England. Andros was governor of the royal colony of New York, won from the Dutch. He ordered the colonies to surrender their charters.

In October 1687, Governor Andros arrived in Hartford with at least thirty-five troops and a court order for the charter. He met with Governor Robert Treat and others at the meetinghouse, but the colonists refused to cooperate. The charter lay on a table between them. Suddenly, the candles in the room were snuffed out. When the wicks were re-lit, the charter had disappeared. According to legend, Captain Joseph Wadsworth took the charter and hid it in a white oak tree on Samuel Wylly's estate. The oak tree stood in Hartford as a symbol of resistance against tyranny until a storm blew it down on August 21, 1856.

The charter was revealed only after King James II was toppled from power in the Glorious Revolution of 1688. Parliament replaced him with his daughter, Mary, and her husband, William of Orange. England became a constitutional monarchy. The power rested in the people through their elected officials in Parliament. The colonies were able to regain their self-rule and overthrow Governor Andros in 1689. The Glorious Revolution was a turning point for England and the colonies, but a stronger Parliament would soon threaten Connecticut's independence.

CHAPTER 3

The Land of Steady Habits

The first spring in the colony of New Haven was so cold that, according to one account in *History of the Colony of New Haven*, "men were forced to plant their corn two or three times, for it rotted in the ground." The colonists had no sawmill, so they had to split logs by hand to build their houses. Some families lived through the winter in cellars with nothing but earth for a roof. Surviving those early years took courage. Far from supplies in the shops of London, families became self-reliant. They felled oak trees and cut the wood for beams for their homes, crafted tools from wood, stone, and metal, cared for the sick, and delivered babies. Every home had a spinning wheel and loom for women to make clothes. When colonists could not accomplish something themselves, they bartered goods for the specialty skills of their neighbors. For example, if one man could shoe a horse and another could build a chair, they exchanged their talents.

Most people in Connecticut farmed their land and raised livestock. With few tools, farmers worked diligently to grow crops to feed their families. Following the Algonquins, farmers used fish to fertilize their farms. Corn was used for food as well as payment for goods. Farmers also grew rye, oats, barley, hemp, and tobacco. Vegetables like beans, peas, squash, onions, and pumpkins grew well in the river valleys. Oliver Wolcott's apple orchard in Litchfield was one of many planted with seeds brought from England. Apple orchards yielded fresh fruit to eat, bake in pies, and press in mills to make hard cider, a popular

Colonial life was extremely difficult due to frequent shortages of food and other supplies. Everyone was expected to work, even children, as seen in this print of girls known as onion maidens working onion fields in the town of Wethersfield, Connecticut. Red onions were extremely valuable during the colonial era. They were often exported as far as the West Indies, England, and the Mediterranean and could easily be used to barter for other items.

alcoholic drink. Every product from the garden was used. Herbs were boiled for medicine. Women wove the fibers of flax into linen. The family's livestock provided sheep's wool for cloth, cows' milk for butter and cheese, and chickens for poultry and eggs.

Products that farmers didn't use themselves, they sold at local markets. Merchants living along the Connecticut River and Long Island Sound owned businesses, land, and large houses. They invested in shipbuilding, loaned money, and held mortgages, for there were no banks in the colony. Eager to profit from the colony's surplus, Connecticut merchants looked to the West Indies, an island chain in the Caribbean Sea.

English settlers with sugar plantations on the islands needed Connecticut's goods to feed their labor, African and Native American slaves. Merchants such as Captain Nathaniel Shaw of

By the 1770s, thousands of slaves lived and worked in Connecticut, providing services for wealthy families and farming the land. This bill of sale from 1766 discusses information related to a nine-year-old slave girl named Venus. See page 55 for an excerpted transcription of the document, which is housed in the Stratford Historical Society in Stratford, Connecticut. Connecticut passed a bill for gradual emancipation of slaves, but slavery was not abolished in the state until 1848.

New London exported wood, livestock, flour, cured hams, fish, pork, butter, vegetables, and wheat to the islands. The ships returned with sugar, molasses, and rum, an alcoholic drink made from fermented sugarcane. At the time, sugar was the most valuable commodity in Europe. Captain Shaw's granite mansion, still standing today, testifies to the fortunes of some merchant colonists.

Tragically, West Indies trade relied on slavery. Men, women, and children were brutally seized in Africa and the Americas, transported, and sold for molasses, rum, or money. Many leaders, such as John Davenport and Theophilus Eaton, owned slaves. Newspapers advertised slaves for sale. Puritans felt that, as God's chosen people, they had the right to use slaves to build the colony. By 1774, Connecticut had some 6,500 slaves plowing fields, driving carriages, and providing domestic service to wealthy families. In 1784, the colony decided that slaves born after 1784 would be free at the age of twenty-five. Slavery was finally abolished in 1848.

Most men in Connecticut were farmers, but many also practiced other trades. They worked as shoemakers, cabinetmakers, weavers, tanners, or blacksmiths. Around 1651, New London welcomed John Prentiss, a blacksmith from Massachusetts. The people built him a house and shop and gave him a half ton of iron and 20 to 30 pounds (9 to 13.5 kilograms) of steel to get started. Clock making became a trade as early as 1638, when Thomas Nash of New Haven built what may have been the first clock in America. More educated men became schoolmasters, doctors, ministers, and merchants.

The gristmill was one of the first colonial enterprises. Gristmills to grind grain were built next to rivers; the mill wheels ran on power generated by moving water. In Wethersfield, a dam was built across Mill Brook in 1635 to run a gristmill. Wethersfield needed the mill to grind grains into flour. Early colonists also harnessed moving water's power to cut wood in sawmills.

In 1648, a Boston shipbuilder, Thomas Deming, was hired by merchants in Wethersfield to build a vessel to sail to the West Indies. Launched in 1649, it held a load of staves, or wood strips, to make shipping barrels. The Colt family built its first shipyard on

Connecticut's oldest gristmill, the Old Town Mill, can be seen in this photograph taken in 1894. Commissioned by Connecticut governor John Winthrop in 1650, the mill was built the following year by John Elderkin. Although the Old Town Mill has since been razed, another of Connecticut's historical mills is located in Mansfield, where it has stood since 1830.

a New London cove in the 1660s. Along the Connecticut and Thames rivers, dozens of shipyards were soon producing sloops, schooners, and other ships. As local economies grew, craftsmen were hired to sew sails, forge iron anchors, and make ropes.

Early Connecticut towns were ecclesiastical societies, with laws based on the Bible. The meetinghouse, often the place where church and educational services were conducted, was the center of social life. Ministers led the community. Everyone had to attend church on the Sabbath, and sermons lasted for hours. Restless children were often punished for misbehaving.

The Puritans had almost no personal freedom. They accepted that every aspect of their lives should be ruled by religion, from the length of a man's hair to the length of a woman's sleeves. Obedience was valued, and those who did not follow the strict rules were punished. They believed that closely following rules gave order to their lives, and allowed families and communities to prosper. Yet these rules also stifled any diversity in the community.

Puritanism lasted longer in Connecticut than in other colonies. One reason was that the colony had laws against people of other religions, including Quakers and Baptists. The New Haven colony passed harsh laws against Quakers. Quakers were sometimes deported from the colony; if they returned, they faced imprisonment, whipping, and branding. One Quaker who stood up against the Southold minister was whipped and branded on the hand with the letter *H*, standing for "heretic," then banished from the colony. Others had their tongues burned with hot irons.

Individuals who seemed different were persecuted, and neighbors often tattled about unusual behavior. Sometimes people blamed eccentricity on witchcraft, a crime punishable by death. Alse Young, a woman in Windsor, was the first person executed for witchcraft in the colonies. Little is known about her life or why she was accused of being a witch. Young was hanged at Meeting House Square in Hartford on May 26, 1647. Massachusetts governor John Winthrop wrote in his journal, "One of Windsor was arraigned and executed at Hartford for [being] a witch." Other women accused of witchcraft were also executed, though some did manage to escape this fate. In 1669, Katherine Harrison, of Wethersfield, avoided death even after a jury found her guilty. After a panel of ministers was asked to establish rules of evidence and procedures for trying alleged witches, Harrison was released.

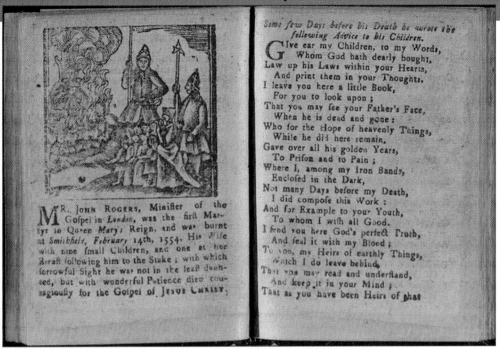

John Rogers (1500–1555), a British Roman Catholic priest who early in his life converted to Protestantism, is celebrated for his martyrdom in this New England primer from 1773. Primers became a staple of American education beginning in the 1690s. They helped children learn to read with a series of woodcuts, each with a letter of the alphabet and a religious rhyme such as, "In Adam's fall, we sinned all." Even two centuries after Rogers was burned alive for his religious beliefs under the order of England's Catholic queen Mary, Puritans were eager to keep alive the prejudice that still existed between Protestants and Catholics in America. This 1773 primer features Rogers's quotations including his dying wish to his children, "Keep always God before your eyes."

Puritan colonists believed in education. They thought children were born sinful and had to learn to restrain their natural impulses. Education taught children to become obedient members of society. Children had to read the Bible and know the laws of their community. In the 1650s, Connecticut passed laws requiring that children be taught to read and be trained in an "honest calling." As soon as towns had 50 families, they had to hire a teacher. With 100 families, they had to maintain a grammar

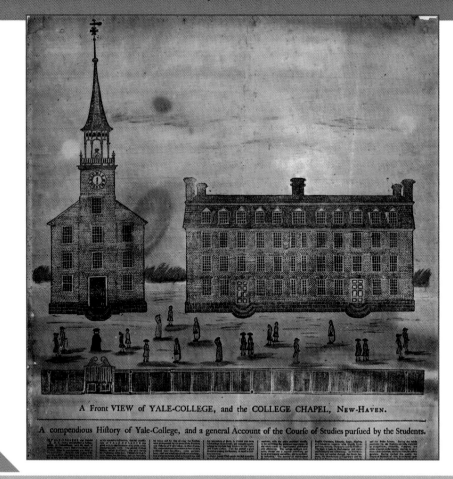

A Front VIEW of YALE-COLLEGE, and the COLLEGE CHAPEL, New-Haven.

A compendious History of Yale-College, and a general Account of the Course of Studies pursued by the Students.

This is the front view of Yale College and its First Chapel as they appeared on the grounds in New Haven, Connecticut between 1717 and 1782. Yale was first founded in 1701, in the home of Abraham Pierson in Killingworth, Connecticut, before it moved fifteen years later to a larger building in New Haven. Artist Daniel Bowen printed this image from a woodcut.

school to prepare boys for future studies, taught by young men usually chosen by ministers.

Stamford built its first school in 1671, with wood from the old meetinghouse, which had partially decayed. Prior to that, children were taught at home by their mothers or in a "dame" school, in which a small group of students were taught by a widow. According to historian Marie Updegraff, the town meeting in November 1670, had decided that Stamford needed a school and voted to "put down all petty scools [that] may be kept in [your] town which may be prejudicial to ye general scoole." By 1700, the General Assembly contributed funds to local schools like Stamford's. Towns were required to educate children aged four to fourteen.

Higher education was also valued. After all, Thomas Hooker and other Puritan leaders had graduated from England's finest colleges. In 1701, a small group of Puritan ministers founded the Collegiate School to educate clergy. The ministers donated books for a library. Students attended classes in the home of its rector, Abraham Pierson, in Killingworth. Elihu Yale, a merchant with the British East India Company, donated 9 bales of goods, 417 books, and a portrait and arms of King George I. The school moved to New Haven in 1716, and was renamed Yale College in 1718. Many politicians, merchants, and judges graduated from Yale College, which became Yale University in 1887.

Connecticut was prospering, but as early as the 1730s, the British parliament began intruding. The Molasses Act of 1733 established a tax of a sixpence per gallon of molasses imported from anywhere except British colonies. In theory, this was a blow to New England merchants who had been importing molasses from the French and Spanish islands in the West Indies, although merchants who had traded in the British-controlled West Indies remained unaffected. By 1750, Parliament had begun to restrict and tax more products. Angry colonists wondered what would happen next.

CHAPTER 4

Revolt Against Tyranny

Connecticut colonists soon felt more pressure from England. By the 1760s, England, led by a new king, George III, faced a financial crisis. The French and Indian War (1754–1763) had left the country deeply in debt. The war gave England dominance over America, but money was needed to manage the colonies, including new land won from the French. British soldiers patrolling the colonies' western borders had to be paid. To raise money, England looked to Connecticut and the other colonies.

In 1764, the British parliament passed the Sugar Act to help solve its financial troubles. The law levied taxes on many foreign goods, including sugar, some wines, coffee, pimento, and calico. The tax on molasses that had been ignored was now strictly enforced. The Sugar Act disrupted the trade with the West Indies. British warships patrolled the Caribbean and North Atlantic, seizing the boats of smugglers. With fewer markets to sell their goods, New London merchants were angry and they protested. Connecticut's governor, Thomas Fitch, published a pamphlet in 1764 against the Stamp Act.

As interference from England increased, the colonists grew resentful. After all, their charter spelled out the right to self-government. Why should they pay taxes set by a government in which they had no voice? "Taxation without representation is tyranny" became the rallying cry of the rebellious colonists.

On March 22, 1765, Parliament passed the Stamp Act, imposing a tax on paper, including legal documents and playing cards. It was the first direct tax on the colonies to be paid to the British crown. Colonists had to pay more for newspapers. Even writing a

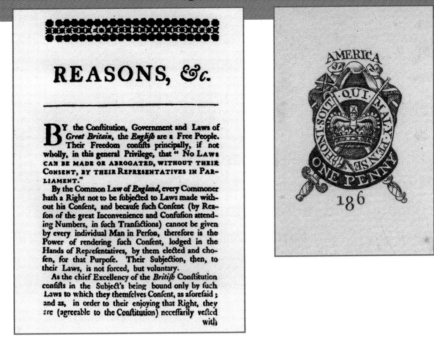

In December 1765, a large group of men assembled in New London, Connecticut, to formally protest the Stamp Act, the new law issued by the British parliament that added taxes to paper goods. The assembly issued a resolution (*left*) that was first published in newspapers such as the *Massachusetts Gazette*. It stated firmly that the newly imposed Stamp Act was "a tax imposed on the colonies without their consent." See page 55 for an excerpt of the resolution. Colonists felt that it was the duty of every person in America to oppose the new tax. This stamp (*right*) is a detail of a proof sheet of one-penny stamps submitted for approval to the Commissioners of Stamps by an engraver on May 10, 1765. Stamps such as this one were used on newspapers, pamphlets, and similar goods that were, according to the British parliament, "larger than half a sheet and not exceeding a whole sheet."

letter required paying for the stamp, but the colonists were more angered by the fact that they were being asked to pay money to the Crown while having no representation in Parliament.

The Stamp Act violated the self-rule guaranteed by Connecticut's charter. Jonathan Trumbull, a leading merchant who would become governor of Connecticut in 1769, wrote to Governor Fitch in August 1765, "The People in this part of the Colony, are very jealous of their Liberties; and desire that the most Vigorous exertions be made for the repeal of the Late Act of

Parliament which they look on to be utterly subversive of their Rights and Privileges both by Charter, and as English Men."

While Governor Fitch had protested the Sugar Act, he felt the colony had to accept the Stamp Act. With four assistants, he stood before the General Assembly and took an oath to uphold the law. Trumbull and others were furious. "It is in violation of your Provincial Oath!" exclaimed Trumbull, who left the room. A year later, voters replaced Fitch with William Pitkin, and made Trumbull deputy governor.

Outrage over the Stamp Act led Connecticut men to organize a local branch of the Sons of Liberty, a secret militia group determined to resist the British. The Sons of Liberty first met at Durkee's Tavern in Norwich. Their leaders were John Durkee, Israel Putnam of Pomfret, and Hugh Ledlie of Windham, all soldiers who had fought with the British in the French and Indian War. Sons of Liberty groups formed in Boston, New York, and other cities. They set out to undermine the British government.

The Sons of Liberty went after Jared Ingersoll, a royal tax collector for Connecticut. Ingersoll's job was to make sure people paid for the hated stamp tax. Protesters surrounded his house in New Haven in September 1765, and demanded his resignation. Fearing for his life, he rode for Hartford to seek protection. But 500 men on horseback, led by trumpeters and militia officers, stopped Ingersoll near Wethersfield. He fled into a house, with the Sons of Liberty in pursuit. Finally, he agreed to resign. They told him to throw his hat into the air and shout "liberty and property" three times, which he did.

The Stamp Act was soon repealed, for the protests caused British merchants to lose money. Still, the colonists worried that England would levy new taxes without their consent. Sure enough, in 1767, the Townshend Act imposed duties on imported tea, paper, glass, lead, and paints.

American Revolutionary War general Israel Putnam (1718–1790) is featured in this portrait in military uniform. Putnam lived in Connecticut from about 1740, and served in the French and Indian War before rising through the ranks to eventually become a major general in the Continental army during the American Revolution. Although Putnam was known to be a courageous and brave fighter and his efforts in 1775, during the Battle of Bunker Hill, gave him great notoriety, within two years General George Washington believed him to be an ineffective leader and subsequently gave him fewer and fewer important duties.

ISRAEL PUTNAM Esq.
MAJOR GENERAL of the Connecticut Forces, *and* COMMANDER *in* CHIEF *at the Engagement on* BUNCKERS HILL *near* BOSTON, *17 June 1775 .*

The final insult was the Tea Act of May 1773, which gave the financially struggling British East India Company a monopoly on tea sales to the colonies. Its tea would be sold inexpensively, undercutting local merchants. Angry colonists turned tea ships away from Philadelphia and New York harbors. In Boston, the colonists would not allow the ships to unload, and the harbor was filled with cargo. On December 16, 1773, members of the Sons of Liberty dressed as Mohawk Indians dumped chests of tea into Boston Harbor. To show their support, the Sons of Liberty in Connecticut burnt tea brought by a peddler to Lyme. More protests followed. Across Connecticut in the summer of 1774, people voted in town meetings to defend American liberties.

Connecticut seethed when the British parliament passed harsh laws in response to the tea protests. Known as the Coercive or Intolerable Acts, these laws closed the port of Boston (the Port Bill), allowed the royal governor to take control of Massachusetts's government, and gave the British the right to house soldiers anywhere in the colonies. In response, the church bells of Lebanon tolled all day and the door of the Town House was draped in black with the Port Bill posted so that everyone could read it. In Farmington, people burned an effigy, or model, of Massachusetts governor Thomas Hutchinson, a Loyalist, and a copy of the detested laws.

To protest the Intolerable Acts, fifty-five men from all thirteen colonies except Georgia met for the First Continental Congress in Philadelphia on September 5, 1774. Connecticut sent Eliphalet Dyer, Roger Sherman, and Silas Deane. For weeks, the men debated how to respond to the harsh laws. On October 14, they issued the Declaration and Resolves, listing their grievances and determination to reject England's authority. The document declared an end to trade relations with England unless the Intolerable Acts were abolished, defined the colonies' rights, and limited Parliament's power.

Governor Jonathan Trumbull began preparing for war. Fearing the British might block the coast, Trumbull ordered the government to "procure 300 barrels of gunpowder, fifteen tons of lead, and 60,000 good flints," according to the Connecticut Society of the Sons of the American Revolution. He appointed a council to direct the war effort and converted his store in Lebanon into a "war office." On March 22, 1775, Trumbull issued a proclamation calling for a Day of Public Fasting and Prayer on April 19. That day in 1775 was the start of the American Revolution.

CHAPTER 5

Sixty-five men gathered at Beer's Tavern in New Haven on a cold night in December 1774. Aaron Burr, the future vice president of the United States, and Benedict Arnold, the famous patriot who would later betray the colonies, were among them. The men formed a military unit called the Second Company Governors Foot Guard. The colonists were at the brink of war with England, and they wanted to be ready to fight.

A few months later, on the evening of April 18, 1775, a column of British soldiers under General Thomas Gage left Boston and marched toward Concord to destroy the colonists' guns and ammunition. Armed colonial militia units, alerted earlier by Paul Revere, met them on April 19. A shot rang out on the Lexington Green. No one knows who fired first, but the British fired on the rebels, killing eight men. The Revolutionary War had begun.

The Provisions State

A postal rider named Israel Bissell set out on horseback to take the news to Connecticut. He stopped in Norwich, New London, Lyme, Saybrook, and, finally, New Haven. His first horse died from riding so hard. Hearing the news, the Second Company Governors Foot Guard voted to assist the rebels. On April 22, Arnold gathered the men on the New Haven Green in full military dress. He requested the key to the king's gunpowder from the city leaders of New Haven. Loyal to the British king, they refused. Arnold forced them to give him the key so that he could get the ammunition. The unit marched to Cambridge, Massachusetts, where some 3,600 Connecticut men soon arrived to fight. In June, the

Second Continental Congress established the Continental army, with General George Washington as its commander.

Burr was trained as a lawyer. Arnold was a successful merchant, trading rum in the West Indies. The Connecticut men who fought in the Revolution were not professional soldiers. They were also teachers, blacksmiths, farmers, and others who left their families and jobs to win freedom. Some were African slaves, who lost half their soldier's wages to their masters. Many went reluctantly, for wartime inflation was high and a soldier's pay was low. At times, Connecticut could not reach its quota of soldiers because families feared they would become destitute without the men at home. Still, approximately 32,000 Connecticut men fought in militia units and the Continental army. Many, like Israel Putnam, made history.

Putnam, a leader of the Sons of Liberty and a tavern owner, was plowing a field in Pomfret when he learned of the Battle of Lexington. He left his plow standing and hurried to Boston to join the patriots. According to the Connecticut Society of the Sons of the American Revolution, his son Daniel later wrote, "He loitered not but left me, the driver of his team, to unyoke it in the furrow, and not many days to follow him to camp." Putnam, who had previously fought in the French and Indian War, was given a regiment to lead.

On June 16, 1775, colonial soldiers marched to Charlestown, near Boston, and began digging ditches and piling hay to fortify Breed's Hill. Putnam led his soldiers to protect nearby Bunker Hill. The Americans were outnumbered when 2,400 British soldiers marched up the hill and British boats in the harbor began firing, but they fought bravely. Putnam shouted, "Don't fire 'til you see the whites of their eyes!" The British suffered many casualties. Some consider the Battle of Bunker Hill a patriot victory, although the colonists retreated after running out of ammunition.

Brigadier General Benedict Arnold (1741–1801) served in the American Revolution until 1779, when he turned on the Patriot forces and sided with the British. Known throughout the years as a colonial traitor after he was passed up for a military promotion, Arnold informed British soldier Major John André about a proposed invasion of Canada and foiled the attack. André was later hanged for his charges while Arnold escaped. In 1781, Arnold led an attack on New London, Connecticut, before fleeing to England.

Colonial leaders began considering how to declare their freedom from England. The Second Continental Congress met in Philadelphia in June 1776. The delegates decided to break all political connection with England. Roger Sherman, a Connecticut leader, was one of five men chosen to draft a document explaining why the colonies should declare independence. They assigned Thomas Jefferson of Virginia to write the words.

In the declaration, Jefferson explained the colonies' complaints against the monarchy and why the colonies should break away. Its central idea was individual liberty, a cherished concept for Connecticut. In July 1776, newspapers across Connecticut published the Declaration of Independence. Four

This letter, written in the hand of General George Washington to Governor Jonathan Trumbull on August 28, 1779, urges Trumbull to get supplies, such as food, for the Continental army. In the missive General Washington tells Trumbull that the army's supply of flour is alarmingly low. Washington and Trumbull often communicated by mail during the Revolution, during which time Washington addressed Trumbull as "Your Excellency."

Connecticut men signed the document—Sherman, Samuel Huntington, William Williams, and Oliver Wolcott. Citizens from Stamford to Litchfield hailed the news of Connecticut's freedom from England's tyranny.

Governor Trumbull was the only colonial governor to support the Patriots and remain in office during the war. He supplied the Continental army with food, salt, gunpowder, and other supplies from Connecticut. Many women were asked to sew clothes for the soldiers. General Washington knew that he could rely upon "Brother Jonathan" for help in the war effort. When Washington's troops were starving during the harsh winter of 1777 to 1778 at

Valley Forge, Trumbull sent a herd of cattle from Connecticut to feed the men. For Trumbull's efforts, Connecticut was nicknamed the Provisions State.

In January 1776, the Council of Safety voted to build a warship to add to Connecticut's growing navy. Uriah Hayden of Essex, was chosen to build the *Oliver Cromwell* in his shipyard in Saybrook (later Essex), equipped with a ropewalk, sawmill, and sail loft. In June 1776, the vessel was launched with a crew of more than 100 men. The ship soon captured the British brig *Honour* with a cargo worth more than £10,000. Meanwhile, New London merchants funded hundreds of privateers, the privately owned armed ships licensed by the colony. Privateers attacked British supply ships and merchant vessels.

No major battles took place in Connecticut, but the British raided the colony several times. On July 5, 1779, British general William Tryon and his men attacked New Haven from the sea, burning buildings and killing many citizens. Days later, on July 12, forty-eight British ships sat off the coast of Norwalk, while 2,600 soldiers led by General Tryon invaded the town. General Washington visited Norwalk ten years later and wrote, "the Destructive evidences of British cruelty are yet visible . . . as there are chimneys of many burnt houses standing in them yet."

In the summer of 1781, the Connecticut ship *Minerva* captured the British ship, the *Hannah*. The *Hannah* was carrying personal supplies for British officers in New York City. The British retaliated. On September 6, 1781, Arnold, now a general in the British army, led 800 British soldiers into New London. The former patriot had betrayed the colonists to join the British after he was denied the title and pay that he felt he had earned. Under Arnold, the British set fire to buildings, wharfs,

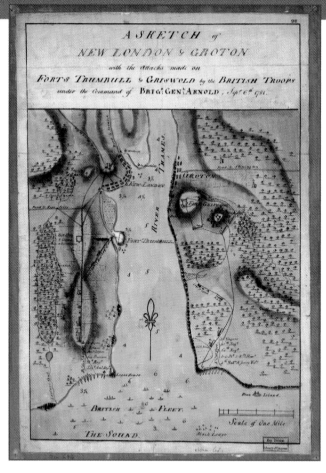

New London, Connecticut, is featured in this pen-and-ink and watercolor sketch while the city was under attack from British forces during the Revolutionary War on September 6, 1781. Forts Trumbull and Griswold are also shown. This sketch is part of the collection of the U.S. Library of Congress.

and ships, sending New London up in flames. Another line of British turned to Fort Griswold, on the east side of the Thames River in Groton. The British captured the stone fort, killing more than eighty colonial soldiers. Fifty-one British soldiers died, and many were wounded. The Revolution left countless scars on Connecticut.

CHAPTER 6

On October 26, 1781, Governor Trumbull wrote in his diary: "About 7 o'Clo[ck] In the even[in]g [received] The hand Bill from D. Govr Bowen, of the surrender of Ld Cornwallis & his Army—9,000 men, Seamen included ..." The British surrender to General George Washington at the Battle of Yorktown on October 19, 1781, signaled the end of the Revolutionary War. Skirmishes between the colonists and the British continued for two more years. The British and colonists signed the Paris Peace Treaty on September 3, 1783, which formally granted America's independence.

The Fifth State

The war was over, but Connecticut's future was uncertain. What would its place be in a newly independent country? How would its voice be heard and its citizens' rights guaranteed? What sort of protections would merchants have in trade and commerce? These difficult questions sparked intense debate in the years to come.

The colonies had been governed by the Articles of Confederation since 1781. This first federal constitution, written shortly after the Declaration of Independence, provided unity under a central government. Yet because the colonies feared giving up too much independence, the Articles of Confederation created a government with limited powers.

A strong national government was needed to support the new nation. Federal guidelines were necessary to collect taxes, regulate trade, negotiate with foreign governments, and enforce similar laws across the colonies. On May 25, 1787, fifty-five delegates from

This engraving, *The Looking Glass for 1787* by Amos Doolittle, illustrates some of the financial issues being debated in Connecticut politics prior to the ratification of the U.S. Constitution. Created in New Haven, Connecticut, the colony is symbolized as a wagon (*top center*) loaded with debts and paper currency, the weight of which caused it to sink into the earth. Its driver warns, "Gentlemen this machine is deep in the mire and you are divided as to its [relief]." The wagon is being pulled in opposite directions by groups of Federalists (those people in favor of taxes) and anti-Federalists (mostly farmers who opposed taxes), each of whom represent different sides of the issues. A stormy sky filled with thunderbolts represents the temperament of colonial politics.

all the colonies except Rhode Island gathered at the State House in Philadelphia to revise the Articles of Confederation. The delegates soon realized that they needed an entirely new constitution to strengthen national unity. At the same time, however, they wanted to protect the rights of the states and the people.

The Connecticut General Assembly sent three delegates to the Constitutional Convention. Oliver Ellsworth was a prominent attorney and judge, and a member of the General Assembly. Serving on the Continental Congress from 1778 to 1783, Ellsworth was a Federalist who favored a strong central government but also supported the rights of the individual colonies. William Samuel Johnson, the son of an Anglican clergyman, was an attorney, educator, and an officer in the Connecticut militia. Johnson also had strong ties with England and the Church of England. In 1779, he was arrested on charges of communicating with the British, but he was later released. During the Constitutional Convention, he chaired the Committee of Style, which shaped the final document.

The third Connecticut delegate, Roger Sherman, represented New Milford in the General Assembly and served as a justice in the Superior Court of Connecticut. Tall, stern, and well spoken, Sherman was known for his integrity and strong religious beliefs. Colonial leaders respected Sherman, who always thought before he spoke. While at the Constitutional Convention, Thomas Jefferson pointed Sherman out to one of his colleagues and said, "That is Mr. Sherman of Connecticut, a man who never said a foolish thing in his life."

The Constitutional Convention had been under way for seven weeks when the delegates hit a deadlock. They could not agree on how the states should be best represented in Congress. Delegates from the large states wanted greater representation, because they contributed more economic and military support to the country. Delegates from smaller states wanted equal representation even though they were home to fewer citizens. These proposals were called the Virginia Plan, or large state plan, and the New Jersey Plan, or small state plan.

Sherman, with support from Ellsworth and Williams, suggested a compromise. All states would have equal representation in the Senate, while representation in the House of Representatives would be based on a state's population. This historic proposal is known as the Connecticut Compromise or Great Compromise. The convention adopted the compromise on July 16, 1787 by a margin of one vote. Without this compromise, Congress would look much different today.

Although the Constitutional Convention ended on September 17, 1787, delegates did not send the draft of the Constitution to the states for approval until October 28. Nine states had to ratify the document for it to become law. Connecticut leaders gathered in Hartford on January 4, 1788, to decide whether the Constitution was good for the state. The State House was unheated, so they met in the Meeting House of the First Society. Spectators filled the galleries. Newspaper reporters took down every word of the debates.

The Constitution was read aloud and each section was debated. No vote would be taken until the document was fully discussed. Ellsworth, a passionate supporter of the Constitution, urged its approval in a speech he gave during a debate in Hartford. He said, "If we wish to protect the good citizen in his right, we must lift up the standard of justice; we must establish a national government, to be enforced by the equal decisions of law, and the peaceable arm of the magistrate." William Samuel Johnson argued that Connecticut's economy was in shambles and needed improvement. Others worried that the power of the federal government would reach too far. General James Wadsworth, a Connecticut militia leader, opposed the government's financial and military power.

During five days of debate, people also raised concerns about the separation of church and state. After all, the laws of

Connecticut were based on religion. On the last day of debate, Governor Samuel Huntington urged approval of the Constitution. "There is at present an extreme want of power in the national government; and it is my opinion that this constitution does not give too much." On January 9, 1788, Connecticut was the fifth state to ratify the Constitution. The vote was 128 in favor, and 40 against.

During its first years as a state, Connecticut strengthened its economy. The colony had a large wartime debt. Paper money issued during the war had almost no value, and many people went bankrupt. Houses and businesses destroyed by British attacks had to be rebuilt. Still, Connecticut struggled less than other states did.

A belief in education, hard work, and political independence, born in the Puritans' early days on the Connecticut River, moved the state forward. Connecticut is small, just slightly more than 5,000 square miles (12,820 sq. km), without much land or natural resources. People turned from agriculture to manufacturing, industry, and education. Mass-production manufacturing was pioneered by Connecticut's Eli Whitney, who designed guns with interchangeable parts, and invented the cotton gin, a device that made cotton profitable. Eli Terry, a clock maker in Plymouth, turned a one-man craft into an industry. He went into business with another clock maker, Seth Thomas. Their factory in Plymouth (later Thomaston) produced 6,000 clocks a year by 1814. Other factories turned out metal buttons, cigars, combs, hats, silk, and cotton textiles.

By 1790, the population of Connecticut swelled to more than 200,000. Turnpike companies developed a road system linking major cities and towns and improving communication.

This engraving of the coastline of Connecticut first appeared as the masthead of the *New Haven Chronicle* in 1786. Connecticut's newspapers stirred up rebellious fervor in the months prior to the beginning of the American Revolution. This engraving is now part of the collection of Yale University Library in New Haven, Connecticut.

Banks were established in Hartford, New Haven, and New London, providing capital for investment. Also, in 1795, Connecticut sold its lands in Ohio and used the $1.2 million to start a Common School Fund, spearheading a statewide public school system. Driven by the values of its colonial founders, Connecticut had a bright future.

TIMELINE

1633 —— Dutch traders build a trading post, the House of Hope, on the future site of Hartford.

1633–1635 —— English colonists from Plymouth colony and Dorchester, Massachusetts, make the first permanent settlement on the Connecticut River, the town of Windsor.

1636 —— Reverend Thomas Hooker and his followers walk from Newtown, Massachusetts, to found Hartford.

1637 —— The Pequot War in Connecticut ends in disaster for the Pequot Indians and leaves Connecticut to the colonists.

1638 —— John Davenport, a Puritan clergyman, and Theophilus Eaton, a wealthy London merchant, found the conservative, religious New Haven colony at the mouth of the Quinnipiac River.

1639 —— The Connecticut colony adopts the Fundamental Orders, providing a constitution and representative government for Connecticut.

1662 —— Governor John Winthrop Jr. obtains a royal charter from King Charles II, setting new boundaries for the colony. The charter is hidden in 1687, when Sir Edmund Andros takes over Connecticut.

1665 —— New Haven officially joins the Connecticut colony.

1775 —— Thousands of Connecticut militia march to Massachusetts for the start of the Revolutionary War. Connecticut provides food, cannons, salt, and other essentials to General George Washington's army.

1776 —— Connecticut's Samuel Huntington, Roger Sherman, William Williams, and Oliver Wolcott sign the Declaration of Independence.

1783 —— The Treaty of Paris ends the American Revolutionary War. England grants the colonies freedom and independence.

1784 —— The Connecticut Emancipation Law provides gradual freedom to African slaves.

1787 —— Roger Sherman, Oliver Ellsworth, and William Samuel Johnson of Connecticut participate in the Constitutional Convention in Philadelphia and suggest the Connecticut Compromise to provide fair representation for the states in Congress.

1788 —— Connecticut becomes the fifth state to ratify the Constitution by a vote of 128 to 40.

PRIMARY SOURCE TRANSCRIPTIONS

Page 14: Excerpt from *A Brief History of the Pequot War: Especially of the Taking of the Fort at Mistick in Connecticut in 1637*

Transcription

Down fell men, women, and children. Those that [e]scaped us, fell into the hands of the Indians that were in the rear of us. Not above five of them [e]scaped out of our hands. Our Indians came us and greatly admired the manner of Englishmen's fight, but cried, 'Match it, match it!'-that is, 'It is naught, it is naught, because it is too furious, and slays too many men.' Great and doleful was the bloody sight to the view of young soldiers that never had been in war, to see so many souls lie gasping on the ground, so thick, in some places, that you could hardly pass along.

Page 17: Excerpt from the Fundamental Orders of Connecticut (preamble and first fundamental)

Transcription

For as much as it hath pleased Almighty God by the wise disposition of his divine providence so to order and dispose of things that we the Inhabitants and Residents of Windsor, Hartford and Wethersfield are now cohabiting and dwelling in and upon the River of Connecticut and the lands thereunto adjoining; and well knowing where a people are gathered together the word of God requires that to maintain the peace and union of such a people there should be an orderly and decent Government established according to God, to order and dispose of the affairs of the people at all seasons as occasion shall require; do therefore associate and conjoin ourselves to be as one Public State or Commonwealth; and do for ourselves and our successors and such as shall be adjoined to us at any time hereafter, enter into Combination and Confederation together, to maintain and preserve the liberty and purity of the Gospel of our Lord Jesus which we now profess, as also, the discipline of the Churches, which according to the truth of the said Gospel is now practiced amongst us; as also in our civil affairs to be guided and governed according to such Laws, Rules, Orders and Decrees as shall be made, ordered, and decreed as follows:

1. It is Ordered, sentenced, and decreed, that there shall be yearly two General Assemblies or Courts, the one the second Thursday in April, the other the second

Thursday in September following; the first shall be called the Court of Election, wherein shall be yearly chosen from time to time, so many Magistrates and other public Officers as shall be found requisite: Whereof one to be chosen Governor for the year ensuing and until another be chosen, and no other Magistrate to be chosen for more than one year: provided always there be six chosen besides the Governor, which being chosen and sworn according to an Oath recorded for that purpose, shall have the power to administer justice according to the Laws here established, and for want thereof, according to the Rule of the Word of God; which choice shall be made by all that are admitted freemen and have taken the Oath of Fidelity, and do cohabit within this Jurisdiction having been admitted Inhabitants by the major part of the Town wherein they live or the major part of such as shall be then present.

Page 23: Excerpt from the Royal Charter of 1662 granted to the colony of Connecticut by King Charles II

Transcription
CHARLES the Second, by the Grace of GOD, KING of England, Scotland, France, and Ireland, Defender of the Faith, &c. To all to whom these Presents shall come, Greeting.

Whereas by the several Navigations, Discoveries, and Successful Plantations of divers of Our loving Subjects of this Our Realm of England, several lands, Islands, Places, Colonies, and Plantations have been obtained and settled in that Part of the Continent of America called New-England, and thereby the Trade and Commerce there, hath been of late Years much increased: And whereas We have been informed by the hirable Petition of our Trusty and Well beloved John Winthrop, John Mason, Samuel Wyllys, Henry Clarke, Matthew Allyn, John Tapping, Nathan Gold, Richard Treat, Richard Lord, Henry Wolcott, John Talcott, Daniel Clarke, John Ogden, Thomas Wells, Obadias Brewen, John Clerke, Anthony Hawkins, John Deming, and Matthew Camfeild, being Persons principally interested in Our Colony or Plantation of Connecticut, in New England, that the same Colony, or the greatest part thereof, was Purchased and obtained for great and valuable Considerations, and some other Part thereof gained by Conquest, and with touch difficulty, and at the only Endeavors, Cadence, and Charges of theirs and their Associates, arced those under whom they Claim, Subdued, and Improved, and thereby become a considerable Enlargement and Addition of Our Dominions and Interest there. Now Know YE, That in consideration thereof, and in Regard the said Colony is remote from other the English Plantations in the places aforesaid, and to the End the Affairs and Business which shall from Time to Time happen or arise concerning the same, may be duly Ordered and Managed, we have thought fit, and at the humble Petition of the Persons aforesaid, and are graciously Pleased to create and make them a Body Politic and Corporate, with the Powers and Privileges herein after mentioned; and accordingly Our Will and Pleasure is, and of our especial Grace, certain Knowledge, and mere Motion, We have ordained, constituted and declared, and by these presents, for Us, Our Heirs and Successors, Do ordain, constitute and declare, that they the said John Winthrop, John Mason, Samuel Wyllys, Henry Clarke, Matthew Allyn, John Tapping, Nathan Gold, Richard Treat, Richard lord, Henry Wolcott, John Talcott, Daniel Clarke, John Ogden, Thomas Wells, Obadiah Bowed, John Clerke, Anthony Hawkins, John Deming, and Matthew Camfeild, and all such others as now are, or hereafter shall be admitted and made free of the Company and Society of Our Colony of Connecticut, in America, shall from Time to Time, and for ever hereafter, be One Body Corporate and politic, in Fact and Name, by the Name of, Governor and Company of the English colony of Connecticut in New-England, in America.

Page 27: Excerpt of a bill of sale for a slave girl named Venus, circa 1766

Transcription

Know all men by these presents that I William Fraser and Rachel Fraser the wife of the said William Fraser of Stratford in Fairfield County in the colony of Connecticut in New England for and in consideration of forty-seven pounds in hand received and well and truly paid by Stephen Curtiss, Jr. of the town and county aforesaid to our full content do by these presents sell let make over fully freely and absolutely bargain set over deliver and confirm unto Stephen Curtiss, Jr. aforesaid and to his heirs executors and assigns for ever one Negro gal of about nine years old called Venus.

Page 35: Excerpt of the Stamp Act resolution printed in the *Massachusetts Gazette*, December 1765

Transcription

By the Common Law of England, every Commoner ha[s] a right not to be subjected to laws made without his consent, and because such consent (by reason of the great inconvenience and conclusion attending numbers, in such translations) cannot be given to every individual man in person, therefore is the power of rendering such consent, lodged in the hands of representatives, by them elected and chosen, for that purpose. Their subjection, then, to their laws, is not forced, but voluntary.

GLOSSARY

abolish To end or outlaw, as in slavery.

charter A written grant by the English monarch creating a colony and defining the rights of the people.

colony A country or area under the control of another country and occupied by settlers of that country.

compromise To come to an agreement by finding a way between extremes.

Connecticut Compromise During the Constitutional Convention of 1787, Roger Sherman suggested that all states have equal representation in the Senate and representation by population in the House of Representatives.

delegate A person who represents the interests of other people.

democracy A system of government in which the people elect their leaders and limit the power of those leaders.

draft To create a preliminary version or plan.

effigy A crude figure representing a person who is disliked.

emancipate To free from the control or power of another.

fortify To strengthen and secure.

Fundamental Orders Connecticut's first constitution in 1639, which defined the principles of representative self-government.

grievance An injustice or cause for distress.

gristmill A mill used to grind grain into flour.

loyalist A person who remains faithful to a government, as in the British Loyalists.

magistrate An official who administers the laws.

monarchy A government led by a hereditary ruler with absolute power.

monopoly Exclusive possession or control of a commodity, like tea.

plantation A settlement in a new country or region.

porringer A shallow metal bowl from which children eat.

privateer An armed ship owned by private individuals holding a government commission and authorized for use in war.

Puritan A member of a Protestant religious group during the 1500s and 1600s that sought to purify the Church of England by returning to the Bible. Thousands fled to the New World to avoid persecution and to found colonies, including Connecticut, based on their religious beliefs.

ratify To formally approve.

repeal To cancel or take away something in a legal action.

sachem A respected leader of a Native American tribe.

Stamp Act of 1765 A tax levied on certain documents passed by the British parliament; it provoked the Revolutionary War.

stocks A device used to publicly punish people who disobeyed laws; a wooden frame with holes for the person's feet and hands.

tax A charge set by authorities on people or property for public purposes.

theocracy A system of government, like that of the New Haven colony, with religious leaders and laws based on religion; government by divine guidance.

tyranny Oppressive power by a government.

FOR MORE INFORMATION

Connecticut Historical Society Museum
One Elizabeth Street
Hartford, CT 06105
(860) 236-5621
Web site: http://www.chs.org

Connecticut River Museum
67 Main Street
Essex, CT 06426
(860) 767-8269
Web site: http://www.ctrivermuseum.org

New Haven Colony Historical Society
114 Whitney Avenue
New Haven, CT 06510
(203) 562-4183

Museum of Connecticut History
231 Capitol Avenue
Hartford, CT 06106
(860) 757-6535
Web site: http//www.cslib.org/museum.htm

Web Sites

Due to the changing nature of Internet links, the Rosen Publishing Group, Inc., has developed an online list of Web sites related to the subject of this book. This site is updated regularly. Please use this link to access the list:

http://www.rosenlinks.com/pstc/conn

FOR FURTHER READING

Doherty, Kieran. *Puritans, Pilgrims, and Merchants: Founders of the Northern Colonies*. Minneapolis, MN: The Oliver Press, 1999.

Fradin, Dennis Brindell. *The Signers: The 56 Stories behind the Declaration of Independence*. New York, NY: Walker & Company, 2002.

Girod, Christina M. *Connecticut: The Thirteen Colonies*. San Diego, CA: Lucent Books, 2002.

Hakim, Joy. *Making Thirteen Colonies*. New York, NY: Oxford University Press, 1993.

Murphy, Jim. *A Young Patriot: The American Revolution as Experienced by One Boy*. New York, NY: Clarion Books, 1996.

Newman, Shirlee Petkin. *Pequots*. New York, NY: Scholastic Library, 2000.

Speare, Elizabeth George. *The Witch of Blackbird Pond*. New York, NY: Bantam Doubleday Dell, 1972.

BIBLIOGRAPHY

Atwater, Edward E. *History of the Colony of New Haven*. Boston, MA: Boston, Rand, Avery & Co., 1881.

Bacon, Edwin. *The Connecticut River and the Valley of the Connecticut*. New York, NY: G. P. Putnam's Sons, 1906.

Bill Memorial Library. "Fort Griswold." Retrieved August 20, 2004 (http://www.billmemorial.org/griswold.htm).

Connecticut Historical Society. "Connecticut History Online." Retrieved July 14, 2004 (http://www.cthistoryonline.org).

Connecticut Humanities Council. "Laptop Encyclopedia of Connecticut History." Retrieved on September 8, 2004 (http://www.ctheritage.org/encyclopedia/encyclopedia.htm).

Connecticut Judicial Branch Law Libraries, "The Code of 1650 or Ludlow's Code." Retrieved September 5, 2004 (http://www.jud.state.ct.us/lawlib/History/ludlow.htm).

Connecticut Society of the Sons of the American Revolution. "Articles About the American Revolution." Retrieved July 9, 2004 (http://www.ctssar.org/articles/index.htm).

Connecticut State Library. "Connecticut Constitutional History: 1636–1776." Retrieved September 9, 2004 (http://www.cslib.org/cts4cc.htm).

Connecticut State Library. "Connecticut History." Retrieved September 8, 2004 (http://www.cslib.org/history.htm).

ConneCTKids. "A Robin's Eye View of Colonial Connecticut History." Retrieved September 8, 2004 (http://www.kids.state.ct.us/history.htm).

Earle, Alice Morse. *Home Life in Colonial Days*. New York, NY: MacMillan Company, 1927.

Fairfield Historical Society. "History of Fairfield—A Summary." Retrieved September 9, 2004 (http://www.fairfieldct.org/history.htm).

Fraser, Bruce. *The Land of Steady Habits: A Brief History of Connecticut*. Hartford, CT: The Connecticut Historical Commission, 1988.

"George Washington's Diary, October 16, 1789." The George Washington Papers at the Library Of Congress. Retrieved March 6, 2005 (http://memory.loc.gov/cgi-bin/query/r?ammem/mgw@field(DOCIDt@lit(wd0552)).

Grant, Ellsworth S. *"Thar She Goes!" Shipbuilding on the Connecticut River*. Old Saybrook, CT: Fenwick Productions, 2000.

Howard, Nora. *Stories of Wethersfield*. Wethersfield, CT: White Publishing, 1997.

Hurd, D. Hamilton. *History of New London County, Connecticut*. Philadelphia, PA: J. B. Lippincott & Co., 1882. Retrieved September 9, 2004, (http://freepages.genealogy.rootsweb.com/~jdevlin/town_hist/nl-chap10.htm).

Mystic Voices. "The Story of the Pequot War." Retrieved September 8, 2004 (http://www.pequotwar.com).

Noah Webster House. "A Short Summary of Noah Webster's Life." Retrieved September 1, 2004, (http://www.noahwebsterhouse.org).

Northeast Magazine, "The State That Slavery Built: An Introduction," Retrieved September 8, 2004 (http://www.ctnow.com/news/local/northeast/hc-slavery.special).

Pomfret, John E., with Floyd M. Shumway. *Founding the American Colonies (1583–1660)*. New York, NY: Harper & Row, 1970.

Shuffelton, Frank. *Thomas Hooker: 1586–1747*. Princeton, NJ: Princeton University Press, 1977.

Trumbull, Benjamin. *History of Connecticut*. New London, CT: H. D. Utley, 1898.

University of Connecticut. "Colonial Connecticut Records." Retrieved September 8, 2004 (http://www.colonialct.uconn.edu).

Updegraff, Marie. "Education Spelled Freedom," in *Stamford Past and Present*. Stamford, CT: Stamford Bicentennial Corporation, 1976.

Van Dusen, Albert E. *Connecticut*. New York, NY: Random House, 1961.

PRIMARY SOURCE IMAGE LIST

Page 9: The title page from *The Bloudy Tenent of Persecution, for Cause of Conscience, Discussed in a Conference Between Truth and Peace*, a book detailing Williams's impassioned plea for religious freedom, was published in London, England, in 1644. It is housed in the Rare Book and Special Collections Division of the Library of Congress in Washington, D.C.

Page 10: Boston printmaker John Foster created this map of New England in 1677. It originally appeared in William Hubbard's book, *The Present State of New England, Being a Narrative of the Troubles with the Indians* (1677). It is housed at the Massachusetts Historical Society in Boston, Massachusetts.

Page 13: An engraving of a Pequot Indian village that was destroyed in 1637, during the Pequot War (1636–1638). This image, called "The Figure of the Indians" was first printed in *Nevves from America*, a book by John Underhill, published in London in 1638. It is part of the collection of the U.S. Library of Congress in Washington, D.C.

Page 14: The title page of *A Brief History of the Pequot War: Especially of the Taking of the Fort at Mistick in Connecticut in 1637*, written by Captain John Mason.

Page 17: The first page of the Fundamental Orders of Connecticut, showing the preamble and the first fundamental. This constitution is housed in the Connecticut State Library in Hartford, Connecticut.

Page 19: Theophilus Eaton, governor of New Haven, wrote the laws for the colony in 1656, the first page of which is pictured. The book of Eaton's laws is housed in the Connecticut State Library in Hartford, Connecticut.

Page 20: The "Brockett Map" of New Haven, circa 1641, shows the placement of its first residencies. The map is housed at the New Haven Colony Historical Society in New Haven, Connecticut. The image of "New Haven's First Meetinghouse," circa 1640, can be found in the Yale University Library in New Haven, Connecticut.

Page 23: The original charter from England's King Charles II to the colony of Connecticut, circa 1662. The charter is housed in the Museum of Connecticut History, Hartford, Connecticut.

Page 26: This early print called "Women Weeding Onions in Wethersfield" is housed at the Wethersfield Historical Society in Wethersfield, Connecticut. It is undated.

Page 27: This letter represented a bill of sale of an African American slave named Venus from 1766. The original is housed at the Stratford Historical Society, Stratford, Connecticut.

Page 31: This woodblock print is from *The New England Primer Improved*, an American primary school text from 1773. This book is housed in the Rare Book and Special Collections Division of the U.S. Library of Congress in Washington, D.C.

Page 32: Artist Daniel Bowen printed this image in 1786, of Yale College and First Chapel in New Haven, Connecticut, from a woodcut.

Page 35 (left): This resolution was written by Connecticut colonists in December 1765, and published in colonial newspapers such as the *Massachusetts Gazette* that same year to encourage opposition to the Stamp Act.

Page 35 (right): This stamp is a detail of a proof sheet of one-penny stamps submitted for approval to the Commissioners of Stamps by an engraver on May 10, 1765. It is part of the collection of the Board of Inland Revenues Stamping Department Archive, the Philatelic Collection of the British Library, London, England.

Page 37: C. Shepard published this print featuring Israel Putnam on September 9, 1775. It was originally published in *The American Revolution in Drawings and Prints* and is part of the British cartoon collection of the U.S. Library of Congress in Washington, D.C.

Page 41: Thomas Hart published this print featuring Benedict Arnold on March 26, 1776. It was originally published in *The American Revolution in Drawings and Prints* and is part of the British cartoon collection of the U.S. Library of Congress in Washington, D.C.

Page 42: This letter from General George Washington to Governor Jonathan Trumbull is dated August 28, 1779. It is housed in the Collection of the George Washington Papers of the U.S. Library of Congress in Washington, D.C.

Page 44: This eighteenth-century map of New London, Connecticut, detailing the British attack on the city during the Revolutionary War is housed in the Geography and Map Division of the U.S. Library of Congress in Washington, D.C.

Page 46: *The Looking Glass for 1787*, an engraving by Amos Doolittle, was created in New Haven, Connecticut, in 1787. It is part of the collection of U.S. Library of Congress in Washington, D.C.

Page 50: This engraving of the coastline of Connecticut first appeared as the masthead of the *New Haven Chronicle* in 1786. It is now part of the collection of Yale University Library in New Haven, Connecticut.

INDEX

About the Author

While researching this book, Ann Malaspina discovered that her mother's ancestors arrived in Connecticut from England in the 1600s. Her great-grandparents lived on a farm in Watertown, where her grandmother attended school in a one-room schoolhouse. Malaspina is a former newspaper reporter and the author of several nonfiction books for young adults.

Photo Credits

Cover © Burstein Collection/Corbis; p. 1 Private Collection/Bridgeman Art Library; p. 7 © The New York Public Library; p. 8 © Bettmann/Corbis; pp. 9, 31 Library of Congress, Rare Book and Special Collections Division; p. 10 Massachusetts Historical Society, Boston, MA, USA/Bridgeman Art Library; pp. 13, 29, 37, 46 Library of Congress, Prints and Photographs Division; p. 14 Courtesy of University Microfilms, Inc. and UMI Company; pp. 17, 19 (left), 23 (top) Connecticut State Library; p. 19 (right) © Getty Images; pp. 20, 50 The New Haven Colony Historical Society; p. 23 (bottom) © Florence Griswold Museum, Old Lyme, Connecticut, USA; p. 26 © Courtesy of Wethersfield Historical Society; p.27 © Courtesy of Stratford Historical Society; p. 32 © Manuscripts & Archives, Yale University Library; p. 35 (left) Connecticut History on the Web; p. 35 (right) Board of Inland Revenues Stamping Department Archive, Philatelic collection, The British Library; pp. 41, 46 Library of Congress, Prints and Photographs Division; p. 42 Library of Congress, George Washington Papers; p. 44 Library of Congress, Maps and Geography Division.

Editor: Joann Jovinelly